The Resume Design Book

How to Write a Resume in College & Influence Employers to Hire You

By
Matthew Cross

BOSTON
LOS ANGELES

Copyright © 2015 by Matthew T. Cross

All rights reserved.

Design, Cover, and Art by Matthew T Cross

Printed in the United States of America

Website: www.resumedesignbook.com
Facebook: www.facebook.com/resumedesignbook
Twitter: @resumebook
Twitter: @bostoncross

For more information and email:
matthew@resumedesignbook.com

ISBN-13: 978-1511873697
ISBN-10: 1511873698

First Paperback B&W Edition April 2015

This book or any portion thereof may not be reproduced or used in any manner whatsoever without the expressed written permission of the author except for the use of brief quotations in a book review.

All characters and stick figures appearing in this work are fictitious. Any resemblance to real persons, living or dead, is purely coincidental.

**For the student
Who dreams that one day
They will find a means
To make their ambitions
A reality**

Mom and Dad, Jenn, Katelyn, Papa, and Family,
Thank you for
your support,
your time,
understanding when I needed space to write,
and being there for me throughout this creative journey.

I love you.

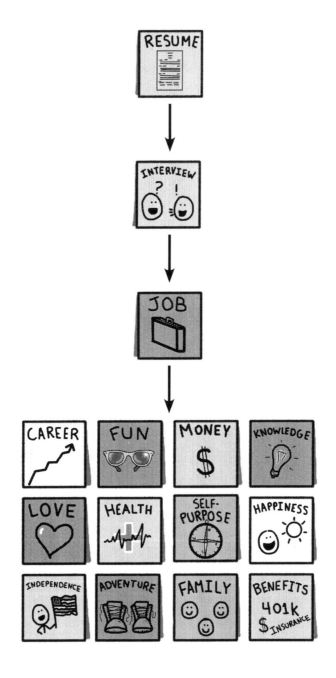

Contents

01 **A Resume Story** — 1
02 **Prototype** — 7
03 **Develop** — 32
04 **Strategize** — 49
05 **Prioritize** — 61
06 **Add Detail** — 70
07 **Format** — 82
08 **Summary Statement** — 94
09 **Feedback** — 100
10 **Review & Submit** — 116

Ten years from now,
how do you imagine your career?

You might imagine yourself as an engineer designing innovative solutions or a scientist finding new cures for diseases. Perhaps you're a teacher or professor, educating future generations of students. Maybe you'll be working in healthcare: sprinting down the hallway of a hospital to save a life. Or...maybe you'll just be the crazy cat lady who "could have done all those things."

Our parents lecture us for years "Start thinking about your future now." We ignore them. Then we ignore them some more, then all of a sudden, reality comes in like a slap in the face. Some of us will rise to the occasion, while others will set expectations that they can't find the path to achieve.

There is no magic genie at graduation granting wishes that dreams become reality, there are just too many graduates and not enough jobs. So, if you want that dream job, you are going to have to earn it. You need to convince that specific employer to believe in you, to hire you, and then to support your development. So how do you turn an employer into a believer?

You can start
by developing
your resume.

"How Do I Start?"

No one creates a perfect resume on their first try, and there is no need to stress yourself out by thinking that you should. Writing a perfect resume is a messy process, but the easiest way to start is by simply getting in the right mindset and putting pen to paper.

Before you write a single word, this book begins with a short story about our fictional hero, Jenny. Jenny's story sheds light on the resume life-cycle. It provides a preview of the process this book will help you to implement on your own.

After you read her story, your first action will be to develop a resume prototype. Think of the prototype as your easiest rough draft possible, or what business professionals call a minimum viable product. It will serve as the foundation for your resume, and will ease the transition to the more advanced improvements unveiled later in this book.

Using this Book

This is not your ordinary resume book. It is designed to make your resume development process interactive, thought provoking, and most importantly, easy to follow. However, to get the most out of your learning experience, you'll be required to use a few tools that challenge the "normal" book experience:

01 Find and keep these handy: a few pads of different colored sticky-notes, preferably Post-It™ brand, and a felt tipped marker or Sharpie®.

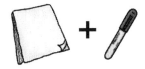

02 Using your smart phone, scan QR codes to enhance your experience with web content that provides more examples, in-depth learning, and inspiration.

03 Pay attention to any "Tips" placed throughout the book. They highlight snippets of important information.

Chapter 1

A RESUME STORY

"Great stories happen to those who can tell them."
- Ira Glass

"Today is the day," Jenny whispered to herself. She sat rigid in her chair, focusing on the laptop screen in front of her. Her mouse pointer hovered over a "SUBMIT APPLICATION" button.

Just as her stomach started knotting and her heart began speeding-up; Jenny forced in a deep breath, closed her eyes, and pressed her finger on the mouse button.

Click.

She did it! When she finally exhaled, her entire body relaxed. Jenny had worked hard for this moment, she just applied for the job of her dreams.

Jenny built her first resume using only a few sticky-notes. Then one section at a time she made incremental changes and her resume quickly improved.

She devised a strategy: tailor her resume to emphasize her employer's needs and not just her own. Studying job descriptions and researching employers helped her determine which of her qualifications matched what they required. She designed her resume format so her reader could efficiently navigate her content, then added detail using evidence based, action-oriented writing.

She gathered feedback from her friends, family, and professionals to help her discover new insights and expose any mistakes in her writing. In the end, the feedback she received helped her make the improvements she needed to feel confident that her resume was ready and motivated her to submit her application.

Fast-forward one week:

Ray, the hiring manager at Fancy Water Corp., began reviewing the applications collecting in his in-box from his latest job posting.

He spent hours at his desk, scanning through a seemingly endless list of resumes. He felt that many candidates had great credentials, but he couldn't find anyone with the right credentials. Just before Ray was about to give up, he read a resume that forced a smile upon his face. The resume glowed with potential.

The candidate didn't have a perfect GPA or an Ivy League education, but their resume expressed, "I'm exactly what you need." It was Jenny's resume.

Soon after discovering her resume, Ray called Jenny for a phone interview. Jenny felt confident talking about the content on her resume and was able to tell engaging stories and provide in depth answers about her experiences relevant to the job she wanted. The interview flowed like she and Ray had known each other for years.

Ray hung up the phone feeling quite impressed. He even got up and made a victory walk around the office. On his way, he stopped by the Human Resources department, poked his head into the directors office, and whispered confidently:

"I found the right one."

Becoming the Right One

How do you think Jenny was able to convince Ray to believe that she was the right one?

It was the methodology she used. A different way of thinking: she approached the problem from the employer's perspective, asking herself "Do my qualifications match the employer's interpretation of value?" By customizing her resume to answer this question she stood out from her competition and successfully communicated that she was the right candidate for the job.

You might find yourself asking, "But what if the job I want places value on skills I don't have yet?" Don't worry, you will learn how to focus on the qualifications you <u>do</u> have. A few missing qualifications won't be enough to deter your efforts, but you should make it priority to attain them. This book's development process will help you organize the qualifications you currently have and help you gain insights into any qualifications you might need to attain for the future.

Chapter 2
PROTOTYPE

Your 12-Minute Resume

"What is a Prototype?"

Today you are a design thinker, and will be building a "prototype." A prototype is the result of an idea being crafted into physical form. They allow yourself and others to see, feel, hear, or smell ideas which are otherwise just a thought in your head. Prototypes are constantly used by designers to gain feedback on how to improve their ideas, and usually start out as a simple sketch or clay model.

A first prototype isn't meant to be organized or polished, and it doesn't even need to represent your final draft. However, it's a great starting point, and for that reason it is how we will begin developing your resume.

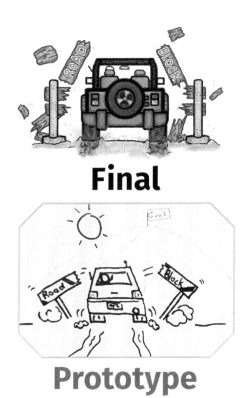

Final

Prototype

The 12-Minute Resume

You are about to embark upon an exercise that breaks down the resume writing process into small manageable pieces. This exercise will help you to transfer some of the important ideas drifting around in your head onto sticky-notes.

All you have to do is remember stories from your life, and write them down one at a time using 12 different sticky-notes. At the end of the exercise you will have all of the building blocks needed to assemble your first resume prototype.

If you've already started writing a resume, great! But don't shrug off this exercise just yet - try it! Inspire yourself to remember what makes you brilliant and unique. You might be surprised at what you've chosen to write down.

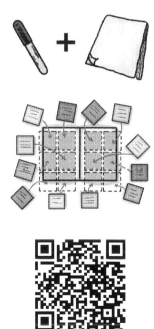

TOOLS

Find a pad of sticky-notes (size: 3.0" x 3.0") and a felt-tipped marker or pen. These are your tools. They will help you write and effectively manage your stories.

You will create tangible sticky-note content to refer back to and use later on in this book. Writing your answers down forces your brain to think differently than it would when typing or simply internalizing your thoughts.

Each sticky note has limited space, so be purposeful with the words you choose. Try not to spend more than 1 minute per note. After 12-minutes you will have a viable resume prototype!

DIRECTIONS

01 Tell your story by filling in the blanks on each page. But instead of actually writing in the blanks, write your answers on a single sticky-note.

02 When you've finished writing your answer: store your sticky-note in the blank square provided.

DIRECTIONS

03 If you mess up, crumple up your note, throw it out, and start a new one.

04 Don't over think your answers. **Just write.**

Ready?

GO!

IDENTIFICATION

My name is _____.

My cell # is _____.

I live in _____.

My e-mail address is

_____.

ABOUT ME

The first three words that come to mind when I describe myself are:

01 _____
02 _____
03 _____

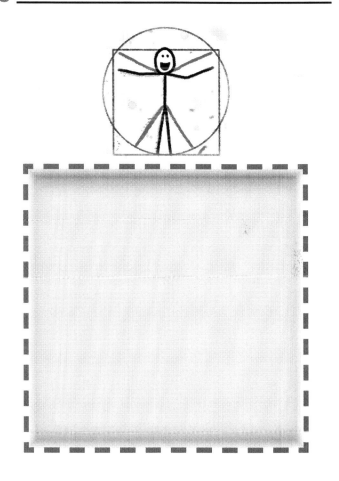

CURRENT GOALS

For me to love my professional job, I need to _____.

EDUCATION

I attend college at _____.

I am working towards a degree in _____.

I plan on finishing this degree in _____.

Subjects / Classes

My top four favorite college courses are (were):

01 _____   **03** _____

02 _____   **04** _____

Project

The goal of my favorite class project was to _____.

I learned _____.

Experience

My job at _____ significantly influenced my career path. I worked there from _____, to _____. My proudest achievement was when I _____.

Computer Skills

The five computer programs that I use in my classes and projects most, are:

01 _____
02 _____
03 _____
04 _____
05 _____

Future Goals

At my 10-year college reunion, I see myself telling my old classmates that my job entails me to _____.

Extracurricular Activities

The three activities, that I enjoy most are

01 _____

02 _____

03 _____

Specific Skills

Three skills I have acquired, that should be useful in my professional career are _____, _____, and _____.

Community

My favorite way to give back to my family, peers, or community is _____.

STOP!

Woooo!

All of that information is now out of your head and on to some sticky-notes where someone else can read it!

ASSEMBLE!

Now, pull off all of the sticky notes that you have filled out and place them in any of the 12 empty spots on the next two pages.

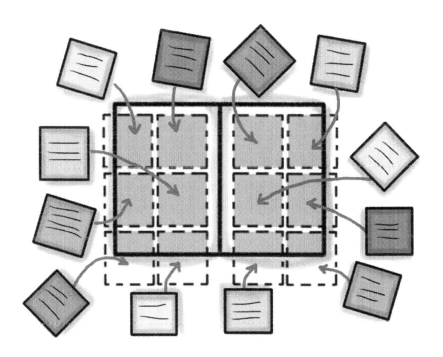

ADMIRE YOUR RESUME!

Look at the story of you! Believe it or not, somebody might want to interview you based on what you wrote in only 12-minutes!

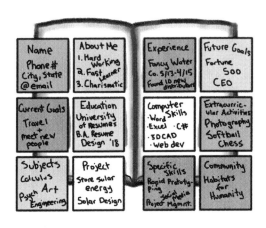

#12MR

"What's Next?"

Some people put off starting a resume for months, even years, because they just don't know where to start. They wait until right before they apply, patch together a resume, and usually end up trying to convince themselves that it's the company's fault when they don't get the results they expected.

In reality, rushing to submit a resume that looks nice but falls short on meaningful content isn't going to get you an interview. You need to learn to think like a resume writer. The purpose of the 12-Minute Resume is to give you something (anything) to build off of. Now we transition into the details of how to improve.

According to Thomas Edison's famous quote "genius is one percent inspiration and ninety-nine percent perspiration," you have now passed into the perspiration phase of writing your resume. Getting the job you really want is going to take some hard work, focus, and dedication. Luckily, the rest of the book is designed to guide you to succeed in that process in a fun and engaging way.

The next chapter will help you to organize the content you've just created into six basic sections, forming the outline you'll use in your final resume. One section at a time you will store your thoughts, expand your story, and become one step closer to having a resume that can open the door to your dream job.

NEXT

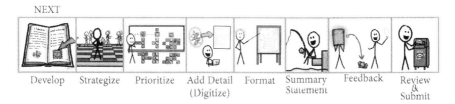

Develop   Strategize   Prioritize   Add Detail   Format   Summary   Feedback   Review
                                    (Digitize)   Statement   &
                                                                               Submit

Chapter 3
DEVELOP

Expanding Your Story

Let's Get Organized!

Now that you have some content (sticky-notes) to work with, we can organize them into groups! The reason we organize content into groups is that it breaks up the overwhelming task of expanding upon content for an entire resume. It allows us to focus on developing one group at a time.

Believe it or not, there are patterns in your qualifications. These patterns form the framework for organizing your existing content into the six basic groups that outline your final copy.

Resume Sections

Below are the six basic sections that every college student should use to organize and outline their resume. It may seem overwhelming, but don't worry; the following development exercise will make it simple! It breaks the groups up, and helps support your development by only needing to focus on one at a time.

01 EDUCATION
02 COURSES
03 PROJECT EXPERIENCE
04 WORK EXPERIENCE
05 SKILLS
06 ADDITIONAL EXPERIENCE

Development Exercise

As you traverse through this chapter, use the examples provided to help inspire you to write your own past and present experiences on new sticky notes. Use the box provided in each section to store your notes. Add to a section by transferring any sticky notes from your resume prototype that fall under each designated group.

Even if you don't think a particular experience will go on your final resume, add it anyways. Sticky notes allow you to visually add, remove, or modify content. Capture everything, open your mind and get it all out. Save making any decisions on filtering out content for later. My challenge to you is to create as many notes as you can.

Education

Think of the education portion of your resume as a high-level summary of the degrees and certifications you are pursuing or have completed. Think back through college and in some cases high school. Consider all of your major achievements throughout your education, especially those that are unique to you.

Your education is important because with only a few words you can show an employer the depth of your potential. When making an internship or entry level hiring decision, smart employers will tend to put more emphasis on how you learn, rather than just what you know.

Use the exercise on the next page to capture information about your education that expresses your professional potential.

 Scholarships can be a really great conversational piece in an interview if there is an intriguing or meaningful story behind why you were selected.

What to Include

For each degree or certificate you are pursuing use a single-sticky note to include the type of degree, college or university, location, GPA (if 3.5 or higher), and expected graduation date. Don't be afraid to break the rules and use two notes if you can't fit it all on one. bachelor

Example:

Add more sticky-notes for:
- Honors
- Awards
- Special enrollment programs
- Scholarships

Include dates and locations as necessary.

Courses

Add as many current and completed courses as possible, dedicating a sticky-note to each one.

Curricula for each specific major vary from college to college. Including courses in your resume will inform your employer of what subjects they can expect you to be knowledgeable of.

Elective courses that are specialized towards a specific field or concentration provide a great opportunity for you to differentiate yourself from your competition.

 On your final resume, for each job that you apply to, rearrange your courses in order starting with the most relevant.

What to Include

Add each course to a new sticky-note. Write down the course number and the full course name:

Example:

Inspiration:
- Biology Courses
- Business Courses
- Computer Science Courses
- Chemistry Courses
- Engineering Courses
- Math Courses
- Language Courses

Project Experience

If you do not have any industry experience or internships, focus on maximizing the value of your projects section. Projects communicate to your future employer that you have the ability to work on complex assignments related to a specific field, just as you would in the real world.

Many degrees require completion of a senior project to graduate, but you can include any project ranging in duration from a few days long to multiple semesters long. Reports, labs, papers, and presentations should all be included in this section. As a college student, this should be one of your most robust and well-developed sections.

What to Include

Assign each project to its own sticky-note, include the class you completed it for, the date completed, and length of time from assignment date to completion.

Example:

Photosynthesis
Lab + Report
BIO-102
2 Weeks
March 2015

Inspiration:
- Senior Projects
- Group Projects
- Individual Projects
- Labs and Reports
- Term Papers or Reports
- Presentations

Work Experience

In this section, include past or present internships and jobs related to your field. These jobs may include teaching assistant jobs, administrative jobs, or any other position relating to your field.

Create detailed content by telling stories about what you did at each job. What were your accomplishments? What were your challenges? What skills did you employ? Separate each story by assigning it to a bullet under your header. Begin each bullet with an action verb describing what you did and follow it with a complete sentence using proper grammatical form and technique.

What to Include

Assign each experience to its own sticky-note, include your job title, employment location, and dates of employment (Start - End). Use the word "Current" as your end date if you're currently employed.

Example:

Inspiration:
- Internships
- Campus Jobs
- Tutor Jobs
- Teacher Assistant Jobs
- Military Jobs
- Self-Employment

Skills

Skills are specific areas in which you have acquired knowledge or expertise. Depending on the job requirements, you will want to tailor the description of your skills by either including more or less detail about each one. For example, if a job requires that you use a specific complex program like Salesforce™, include more details about your knowledge of the inner-workings of that program and how you might use it. Depending on the importance of the skill to the employer, you can either use subheadings under a general "Skills" heading, or create specific skill headings, like "Computer Skills".

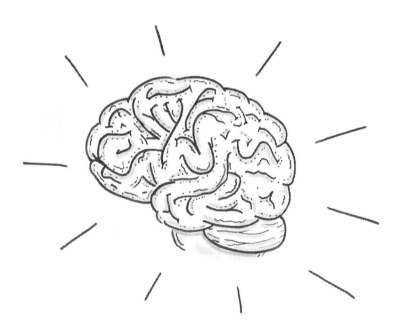

What to Include

Add each skill to a new sticky-note. Write down the specific skill and the group of skills it falls under; create a hierarchy on each note ranging from very general to as specific as you can get.

Example:

Inspiration:
- Language Skills
- Computer Software Skills
- Design Skills
- Lab Skills
- Healthcare Skills
- Writing/Editing Skills
- Manufacturing Skills

Additional Experience

The additional experiences section is where you put all of the information about yourself that doesn't quite fit into the other sections. The purpose of this section is to tell your employer, "This is what I do with my free time". It is a great opportunity to showcase your individuality and differentiate yourself from other candidates. Employers know that many of your experiences outside of work and school have an influence on your personality and professional characteristics. Add them to show leadership, creativity, commitment, or other qualities that will make you successful in the workplace.

What to Include

Assign each additional experience to its own sticky-note. Include dates and locations as frequently as possible.

Examples:

Inspiration:
- Extracurricular Activities
- Clubs and Organizations
- Interests, Hobbies, and Talents
- Fraternities, Sororities, or Societies
- Volunteer Work
- Social / Networking
- Sports Teams
- Events

Invest in your Future

There is a secret that separates those who go on to have successful careers and those who do not. Those who succeed know that getting a job takes work! The more effort and time that you put into your resume and professional development, the closer you will get to having a career you love. This book provides the tools, but it is up to you to maximize their value and make them work for you.

If you had trouble with this last exercise, dig deeper into your personal records. Pull out binders, print out e-mails, and obtain past course syllabuses. Collect as much information as you can about each section so that you have more choices to select from for your final resume. This exercise doesn't stop here. Add to it over the next week, month, or year and you will soon have an overflowing assortment of qualifications.

Chapter 4
STRATEGIZE

Employer Empathy

The "Interview" Folder

Employers want their final decision to feel easy, but sometimes receive an overwhelming number of resumes for a single job offer. To optimize their selection process, employers often scan resumes searching for attributes they either like or don't like about a candidate. An employer then filters candidates into one of two locations. The candidate will either make it into the interview folder or be placed into the save for later (never to be seen again) folder. Our goal is for you to make it into the interview folder.

Become an A+ Candidate

Sending the same copy of your resume to every job you apply for, or "the shotgun method" as some like to call it, is not the most effective way to get the job you want. To increase your chances of getting hired, customize your resume for each new job application. This strategy may keep you from applying to a large number of jobs, but it will help you get an interview for the ones you really care about.

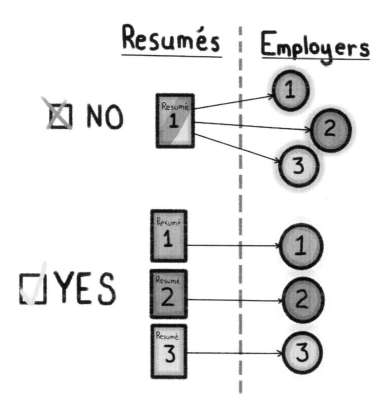

Learn About the Job

The fastest way to learn about a job is by understanding its job description. Job descriptions are written by an employer to explain goals, job details, and the specific qualifications they expect from a candidate.

Job descriptions are located within employers' job postings. Job postings can be found on company websites, at your college career center, or through career search websites like collegerecruiter.com, experience.com, and college.monster.com.

Instead of guessing what an employer is looking for, use the following exercise to be sure of what to focus on.

Job Research Exercise

Find a job description for a single job to which you'd be interested in applying.

As you read through the description, take note of any qualifications, skills, or personality traits the employer is looking for. Also try to uncover any needs they might subconsciously infer using clues in their writing. For example, travel requirements may mean you need your own car or means of transportation available. Using two different colors of sticky notes, write the requirements that you possess using one color, and the requirements you need to improve upon or attain using the other. Store the sticky-notes you fill out in the box provided below.

Learn About the Company

Different companies have different qualities. Some companies minimize risk, follow strict rules, and employ bureaucratic processes. They look for employees who work well within a structured environment, follow rules, and avoid mistakes. Other companies are looking for creative minds that aren't afraid to take risks and discover new opportunities to gain an edge on the competition.

Think of the job market as a spectrum on which these examples lie on opposite ends. Where does the company you are applying to fall on the spectrum? Will you be an instant fit, or will you have to adapt?

Answering the questions on the next page will give you more insight into the range of employer needs to which you can match your experiences and promote them on your resume. Not everything about an employer is specifically communicated in the job description, so you will also have to use other resources to learn about their business.

Company Research Exercise

Research opportunities:
Internet search engines, company websites, news, blogs, social media, and the company's products

Questions to answer:
01 What industry are they in?
02 How they earn capital (money)?
03 Who are their customers?
04 Who are their competitors?
05 What is their mission statement and business model?
06 What do their employees all have in common?

55

Your Future Employer

It takes years of experience and dedication to be in a position to hire an employee. Companies can't afford to make hiring mistakes; they only let people they trust make their hiring decisions. The person reading your resume knows what qualities to look for, because they embody those qualities themselves.

When hiring a new employee, managers don't like to take risks. Hiring the right employee is as important to them as finding the right job is to you. They are accountable for whether or not the employee they hire is able to do the job they are assigned, be a team player, and represent themselves positively in the workplace. They know their own job depends on it.

They think of a job as a privilege, and not as a right. To an employer, each employee has to provide more value to their company than they take away. Putting this concept into perspective: if every employee cost a company more than the revenue each generated for that company, the company wouldn't survive. The funding that keeps them employed would cease to exist.

Thinking like an Employer

Take time to safely perform the following exercise throughout your resume writing process:

01 Find a comfortable place to sit and close your eyes. Disassociate yourself from the resume content you've written; pretend it is no longer yours.

02 Next, while your eyes are closed: imagine yourself as the employer who wrote the job description. You are only going to hire one new person over the next five year period, and you want that person to be someone you believe will do the job well.

03 Feel yourself transform into the employer, then open your eyes and read your resume content.

04 As the employer, note which content is important to your hiring decision, and which content isn't.

When you jump back into your own shoes: know that your resume doesn't have to be perfect, but you can use what you've learned from this exercise to adapt your resume to be as desirable as possible for the employer you imagined yourself to be.

Qualifications Perspective

Employers list skills and qualifications they are looking for in job descriptions, but just because you don't have all the qualifications listed doesn't mean you won't get the job.

Many times employers have trouble communicating exactly what they are looking for in a job description and how they might favor certain qualifications over others. A candidate could only have 80% of the qualifications listed, but can get still the job over someone who has 90%. Don't become discouraged or hesitate to apply to a job just because you don't perfectly match every qualification. You still have a chance if you match and excel in the important ones..

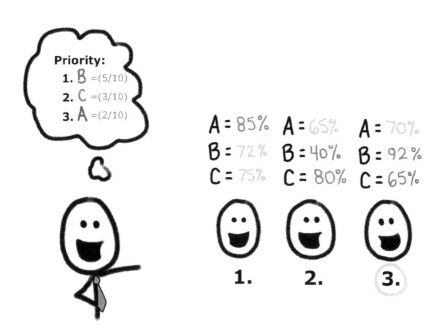

Establish Your Story

The truth is, we all love stories. We tell stories around our friends, at parties when we meet new people, and around the dinner table with our family. Just like the plot to a great novel, resume stories help effectively connect you with your reader or potential employer.

Stories trigger feelings that force an employer's brain to think, in turn, making you more memorable. Values, adversities, and nostalgia are all emotional criteria that employers can connect with. Finding a way in your resume to connect an employer with your story can have a significant effect on their hiring decision.

Plan Ahead for the Interview

During most professional interviews, the interviewer has little knowledge about who you are. What they read on your resume will likely be the only information that they know about you.

There won't be enough room to share entire stories on your resume, but you can customize your resume to provide previews to them. Do this by promoting content that, if asked about in an interview, can be supported by a juicy story. This will help you communicate deeper meaning behind how you apply your skills, and will help your employer better grasp who you are and what you're capable of.

I guarantee that at some point in an interview, the interviewer will use your resume as a guideline to ask you questions about your past experiences. When those question arises, you can use your stories to make the interview feel more like chatting around a campfire, and less like getting grilled in an interrogation room.

Chapter 5
PRIORITIZE

Your resume, like a chain, is no stronger than it's weakest link

Prioritizing Your Content

Hopefully your book is so full of sticky notes that you can barely close it. However, all of this content is going to need to fit on just one side of one page in your final resume. So, you'll need to be picky about what to include or exclude.

The upcoming exercise will help you prioritize and choose your content using our initial strategy: become an A+ candidate and design your resume around an employer's wants and needs.

You may have to make some tough choices, but it is important to remember: the content you exclude can be just as important as the content you include. Promote what you want your employer to read and remove any distractions or risks.

Selecting Content

It's time to start breaking out of the book! The following exercise is going to ask you to visually display all of your sticky-notes from *Chapter 3: Development* onto a large blank workspace. Then you'll decide based on your job research and company from *Chapter 4: Strategize*, which content to include or exclude on your resume. You should perform this exercise each time you apply for a new job to help you customize a specialized resume for each.

Visual Selection Exercise

01 Find your creative canvas:
Secure a blank wall, white board, or window on which to visually display all of your sticky-notes.

02 Define Filter Goal (in the form of a question):
"How valuable is this content to the employer?"
Write this question on a new sticky-note and post it in the center of your working space, slightly above eye-level.

Visual Selection Exercise

03 Create selection filters: using three new sticky-notes, label your filters *EXCLUDE, UNSURE,* and *INCLUDE*. Post them on the wall just below your goal, about 3-feet away from each other.

04 Create six new sticky-notes each representing a resume section for all three filters (18 new sticky notes in total). Post them up on your workspace.

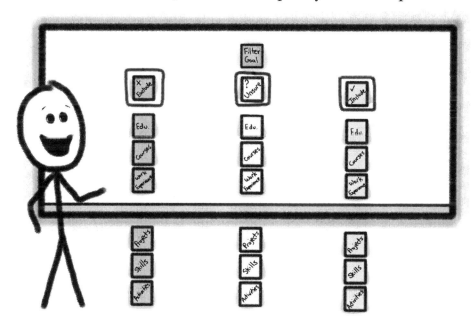

Visual Selection Exercise

05 Post the sticky-notes you created for each section from *Chapter 3: Develop* up on your workspace.

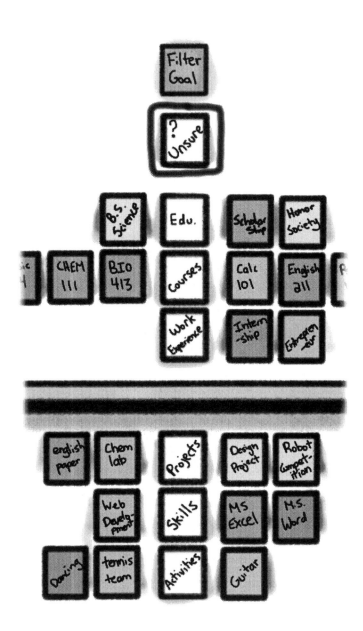

Visual Selection Exercise

06 Move and re-organize your sticky-notes to where you think each one belongs on the board. Address each sticky-note on the wall one by one: Should you include it, exclude it, or are you unsure you want it in your final resume? Use what you've learned in your job description and company research from *Chapter 4: Strategize* to help you decide.

Trust your gut. It is OK to leave sticky-notes in the unsure filter if you don't feel confident about whether to keep it or leave it out.

Visual Filter Review

Use the content you've moved under the *INCLUDE* filter in your final resume. Similarly, overlook any content you moved under the *EXCLUDE* filter.

Wait to decide what to do with the content left in the *UNSURE* filter until **Chapter 9: Feedback**. When the time comes, get feedback from other sources about whether they think you should or shouldn't use it in your final resume.

TIP! Take a picture of your entire workspace "as-is" and save it before tossing any sticky-notes in the recycling bin.

Computer Time!

Finally! Turn on your computer. Open a word processing program. Type out each of your resume sections: Education, Courses, Project Experience, Work Experience, Skills, and Additional Experience. Add the content from the notes you wish to include beneath each appropriate section heading.

Example:

Work Experience
   Fancy Water Corp, Newton, MA, 2013-Current
      Sales Associate
   Computers'R'Us, Newton, MA, 2012-2013
      Customer Service Representative

Chapter 6
ADD DETAIL

Earn Believers

Introduction to Writing

Adding detail to your experiences, projects, and skills takes basic writing skills and a good memory. The goal of adding detail is to give your reader a closer look at the "who, what, where, when, and how" of your experience. By answering those basic questions you can creatively devise a generous number of possible answers.

Write an explanation for each piece of experience in a full sentence with a period at the end. Use the following Resume Detail Do's and Don'ts to help you construct your detail.

Don't spend too much time worrying about a specific format, as that will be discussed in the next chapter. By the end of this chapter your resume should look something like this:

Sample Un-formatted Resume

Get Writing!

As you add detail to each experience, keep your sentences short. Each sentence should be no longer than one line, and should have its own indented bullet point. Use the following list of directions to help inspire direct and meaningful content.

Resume Writing Do's

01 **Ask yourself questions**
02 **Start with an action verb**
03 **Use appropriate tense**
04 **Use facts**
05 **Use numbers**
06 **Be aware of specificity**
07 **Be purposeful**
08 **Check grammar & spelling**

Find Inspiration!

It's time to start thinking like a writer. In order to help you remember your experiences, ask yourself the following questions to come up with value-added detail.

Inspiring Questions

01 What was the goal of my experience?
02 What was the most important thing I learned?
03 What was the most difficult thing I did?
04 What was the easiest thing I did?
05 What part of my experience will be most useful in my future employment?

Start with an Action Verb

Engage your readers by starting sentences and statements with action verbs. Starting a statement with an action verb immediately signifies that you actively "did" something. Employer's eyes will gravitate towards action because that is what they are interested in: what you can "do". When your writing becomes action oriented your reader becomes more motivated, you can hold their interest longer, and you'll induce a slight amount of good stress on that person (making you more memorable).

Examples of Action verbs:
- Designed...
- Managed...
- Tested...
- Maintained...
- Analyzed...
- Evaluated...
- Influenced...
- Consulted...
- Collaborated...
- Improved...

Use Appropriate Tense

Properly communicate past vs. present tense. Has the experience already happened or is it something in which you are actively participating in? Tense-related mistakes in your resume will force the reader to stop and will confuse their mental time-line. Things you are currently working on must be written in present tense. Things you have already completed must be written in past tense.

- **Present Tense (**correct**):**
    I am _designing_ a time portal _today_!

- **Past Tense (**correct**):**
    I _designed_ a time portal _yesterday_!

- **Mixed Tense (**incorrect**):**
    I am ~~designing~~ a time portal ~~yesterday~~!

Use Facts

There are two types of writing you will use in your resume: objective and subjective. You should use both. Subjective writing is something that anyone could argue or debate. Objective writing emphasizes facts and figures and devoid of opinions or personal beliefs.

Your resume is a formal and professional document, which generally means it should be read in objective style writing. Depending on the job however, your employer doesn't expect you to be a robot. You can add value to your resume with quality subjective statements. When using a subjective statement, make sure you can defend it through your experiences, skills, or activities.

Try to limit using of words that can't be quantified, for example: any, each, few, many, much, most, several, some, nobody, somebody, or something.

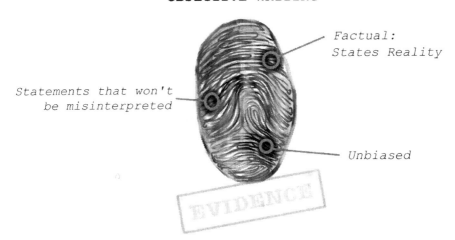

OBJECTIVE WRITING

Factual: States Reality

Statements that won't be misinterpreted

Unbiased

Use Numbers

Numbers provide tangible results and accountability from your experiences to which employers can relate. However, identifying when, where, and how to use numbers effectively can be difficult to master.

The simplest way to know where to use numbers is to find and mark all of the places where an employer might ask: "how much?" (Money), "how many?"(Amount), and "how long?"(Time).

Some important rules for how to use numbers are:
- Avoid starting sentences with numbers
- Avoid putting two numbers next to each other (2 10 person teams or 3 12 hour days).
- If the amount is smaller than 10, spell it out (Supervised seven employees), otherwise let it rip and annotate accordingly ($12,500, 1,050%, 14°F).

Be Specific

Specificity is a technique that promotes clear and particular communication, leaving little room for misinterpretation. Being specific will help differentiate you from other competition. It shows that you have an advanced understanding of the qualifications that you choose to be specific about in your resume. If a job description requires you to be an expert at using a piece of software, don't be afraid to share what specific aspect of that software you are most familiar with.

Example:
CAD -> Solidworks -> Sheet metal Design -> for commercial products

Use specificity to your advantage; varying how general or specific your qualifications are based on a job's requirements. A CAD program can represent multiple types of similar software. It could mean you know Solidworks, Pro-E, or Autodesk. An employer may be familiar with one program, but not the one you know. In this case, be more general about how you describe your knowledge, and an employer may be willing to invest in hiring you, with the expectation you can translate your knowledge to the program they use.

Be Purposeful

To add purpose to your writing: design your content to have the most impact with the fewest number of words. Have a reason for each word and its placement in a sentence. Your reader doesn't have time for indirect resume content or extraneous information.

Remember the "develop" and "prioritize" exercises from Chapters 3 and 5? Following that trend, write as much as possible at first, then select and use the most relevant content for the job to which you are applying.

You may have to re-write a sentence 10 different times to find the best way to communicate your experience to your reader. The effort you make to add purpose to your writing will be well worth it when your resume makes the cut.

Check Grammar & Spelling

Many employers consider spelling errors and improper use of grammar to be a hiring risk. They want to be represented by employees who can effectively communicate to both co-workers and customers. Your resume will be used as a writing sample to judge your communication skills.

Seek out and fix grammar and spelling errors so your reader can focus on your content and not on your errors. Depending on how tolerant the reader is, mistakes in grammar and spelling may result in someone else being hired over you.

Do the best you can, then hire a professional to proofread your resume. You will learn more about how to do this in Chapter 9 - Feedback.

Common Grammar Mistakes to Avoid:
01 Run-on sentences
02 Confusing Tense (Past, Present, Future)
03 Misplaced modifiers
04 Incorrect subject / verb agreement
05 Improper use of apostrophes

Minimize Risks

Avoid certain language triggers that harmfully impact your credibility. Even the best candidate can be passed over if the reader negatively interprets the language used.

Resume Writing Dont's

Don't Use slang. It's not professionally cool, dude.

Don't Use "I." You are the assumed subject of the resume. The subjective pronoun "I" becomes repetitive and inefficient.

Don't Be repetitive. Switch it up! Avoid using the same action verb more than once, keep your reader engaged.

Don't Use big words. Sesquipedalian words can confuse a reader and interrupt their flow. The best communicators use words that are easily understood by others.

Chapter 7

FORMAT

Your qualifications map

Format Creativity

An effective resume format systematically directs your reader to the information you want them to read in the most efficient manner possible.

This chapter introduces the variables for the standard functional resume (with an added little twist of course). These variables serve as a guideline to help you customize the format of your resume. Use these guidelines to plan a format that fits your personality, justifies your value, and catches your future employer's eye.

BE PROFESSIONAL,
BUT DON'T BE
AFRAID TO FOLLOW
YOUR CREATIVE INSTINCTS.

Format Variables

The following variables should be considered when designing your resume format:

01 Page Layout
02 Organization
03 Identification
04 Content Location
05 Font Size and Style
06 Bullet Size and Style
07 Spacing
08 Number of Words

Use the format example on the next page to identify each variable. Following the example are eight pages that explain each variable in detail. These pages will help you to independently design and organize a format that reflects your content best.

Format Example

Full Name
Cell Phone Number
e-mail@address
Town/City, State

Summary
A concise but powerful statement describing who you are, what kind of work you are interested in, and why you are qualified for a job. You will know it is good when you tear up while reading it.

Education
Degree Type and Field - College/University - Location - Date/Expected Date of Graduation
Honors - Awards - Example: Deans List, Honor Society, Eagle Scout, Class Ranking
Scholarships that were granted to you for a reason that would impress or attract an employer

Relevant Work Experience
Employer - Location - Title - Dates of Employment
- Add descriptive statements that explain your accomplishments, challenges, and efforts.
- Show that you learned and used specific skills required for the job you are applying to.
- Begin each statement with an action verb to show your reader that you actively did something.

Courses
List full course names for completed or current courses that relate to the job you are applying to.

Projects
Project Name - Course Name - College/University - - - - - - - - Dates of Project Commitment
- Include examples of projects, labs, reports, papers, or presentations that relate to a specific job.
- Add descriptive statements that explain your accomplishments, challenges, and efforts.
- Show that you learned and used specific skills required for the job you are applying to.
- Begin each statement with an action verb to show your reader that you actively did something.

Skills
Skill Type: Details and examples of knowledge related to skill type.
Skill Type: Details and examples of knowledge related to skill type.
Skill Type: Details and examples of knowledge related to skill type.
Skill Type: Details and examples of knowledge related to skill type.

Other Work Experience
Employer - Location - Title - Dates of Employment
- Add descriptive statements that explain your accomplishments, challenges, and efforts.
- Show that you learned and used specific skills required for the job you are applying to.
- Begin each statement with an action verb to show your reader that you actively did something.

Activities
Name of activity, interest, hobby, volunteer work, club, or society - - Dates of Commitment
- Add action oriented statements showing how you learned career related skills.

Sample Formatted Resume

More Samples

Page Layout

Your entire resume should fit on one side of a single 8 ½" x 11" page, oriented in a portrait layout. Readers use the beginning and end of lines as reference points for navigating a page and feel more comfortable reading the shorter lines of a portrait layout.

The top of the page should have a ½" margin. The standard is a 1" margin, however reducing this to ½" puts your name a little higher than the rest of your competition, a sweet little mind trick to make you stand out. The page should have ½" margins on the left and right side, and a 1" margin on the bottom.

Example:

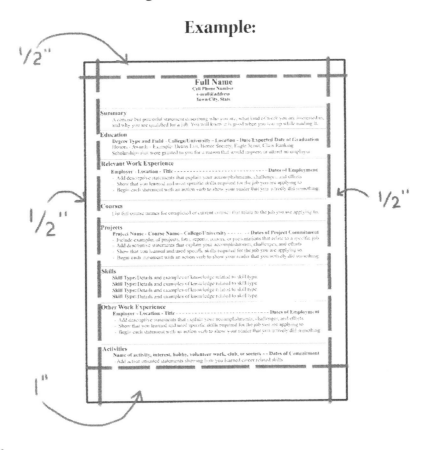

Identification

The most important part of your resume is your reader's ability to identify who you are and how they can contact you. You want to make sure they remember you. Force the issue by making your name the easiest thing on the page to reference. Do this by identifying yourself in a header at the top of your resume.

Think of your identification heading as an introduction or a handshake. Put your reader at ease and immediately let them know who you are, where you live, and how to contact you (e-mail address and phone number).

Not everyone will have the same heading. If you think it will help your chances of getting a specific job, you can get creative by adding your social media profiles or a website address if you have one.

Example:

Be cautious if you put this information in the document's "Heading." If at some point you are required to copy/paste your document into a form, you want to make sure your identification is included in the content you select.

Content Structure

A simple and well-organized resume format minimizes distractions, calms the reader, and gives them a more flexible attitude towards your content.

Think of your organization as if it were structured like a tree. Starting with the trunk, "My Resume" is the theme from which you will branch out. Next, form larger branches for your sections. Then, each section will have a series of small branches designating more specific experiences and details.

On your resume, style your font to gradually get bolder and bigger as you approach the trunk. This technique will help your reader to visually identify key areas, navigate your content, and make it easier to find the location of any content they wish to return to.

Content Location

Be mindful of where content is positioned on your resume. Visualize a heat map when you are deciding where to put each piece of content. Traditionally, people read left to right and top to bottom. Given that constraint, follow this simple rule of thumb: the top left zone of your resume holds the most value. Value then decreases as you approach the bottom right zone. Put your "must have" content in the hot zones and your "nice to have" content towards the cool zones.

When deciding where to place your content, ask yourself: "Why should I dedicate this space to this piece of content and not another?"

As a young professional, your education is a very important. It should be the first section your hiring manager reads. Locate it directly below your summary statement.

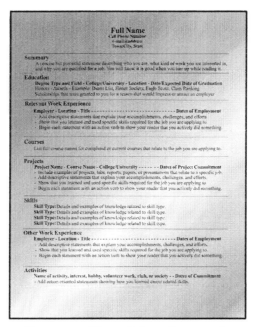

Resume Heat Map Example

Font Type

When applying for a professional job, the font that you choose should express a professional persona. Your font type and styles should be easy to interpret. Fonts that are visually straining can hinder a reader's comprehension and should be avoided at all costs. If you are submitting a physical copy of your resume, **Serif** fonts make your letters more distinctive and are easier to identify while reading on paper.

For digital copies, use a **sans-serif** font. They will look cleaner and be easier to identify than serif fonts at lower resolutions. Most computer monitors won't achieve the resolution (dpi) of a quality printed page and can make serif fonts appear blurry to your reader.

Try some different fonts and decide for yourself which best represents your personality.

- Book Antiqua
- Georgia
- Times New Roman

- Arial
- Calibri
- Vrinda

- ~~Comic Sans MS~~
- ~~STENCIL~~
- ~~Script~~

Organization Techniques

Indentations and bullets are a great formatting tools to break up and organize large groupings of content.

Use paragraph indentations as an organizational tool to help direct your reader among large chunks of content. Use indentations like a file structure on you computer: indent each line further if it refers to a larger heading prior.

Using bullets to separate statements lets the reader know when the subject is changing. You can use multiple sentences with the same bullet, but they should all relate to the same context. Try to fight your creative urges and keep your bullet type simple.

Spacing

Many resume professionals preach about white space, but large blank areas make your resume look uneven or starved. Use proper spacing to fill your page, create top to bottom symmetry, and keep your resume aesthetically pleasing.

Use double spacing when breaking up sections of your resume. This lets the reader know they are at a break. Use single spacing when you want to link similar pieces of content together. This lets the reader know they are reading a continuation of a larger topic.

You can also use double spacing as a way to separate large chunks of content. For example, use double spacing before and after sections to let your reader know where each begins and ends.

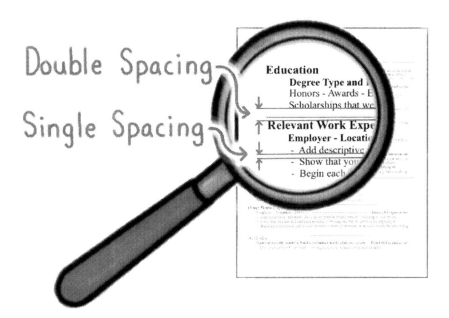

Word Count

Keep your resume word count between 300 and 400 words per minute. Employers will read at a speed of about 400 words per minute, and should be able to read your entire resume in less than 1 minute. The sample resume used on page 85 has 340 words. You will notice that 340 words fill the page nicely.

For more perspective:

If the average time spent reading a resume is 20 seconds, that means (450*(20/60) =) 150 words is the optimal number of words for an employer to read your entire resume.

Chapter 8

SUMMARY STATEMENT

Hook, line, and sinker.

Your Resume "Sales Pitch"

Those commercial sales personalities may seem a bit goofy on TV, but they know how to put together one hell of a sales pitch. If an employer gave you an opportunity to convince them to hire you using only one sentence, what would you say? In essence, adding a summary statement to your resume is your opportunity to say it.

A summary statement is a concise, but powerful statement at the beginning of your resume used to introduce you to your reader and convince them you are the right person for the job.

A few reasons to have a summary statement in your resume:

- Grab your reader's attention and motivate them to read more about you.
- Confirm that your skill-set and interests align with the job to which you are applying.
- Highlight your most valuable qualifications.
- Differentiate yourself from your competition.

Approach and Structure

You want to be able to reinforce your statement with supporting details in your resume without sounding repetitive. It should not sound like a list of buzzwords, but rather a coherent and well structured collection of sentences. Your statement should generally be objective, but can be supported by subjective components with emotional context or personality traits. However, any subjective claims you make should not be misleading. Promote the qualities which best represent who you are in real life.

Your statement can be broken up into 2-3 sentences. However, it should only take up 2-3 lines on your resume. Your statement should be easy to read and roll off the tongue easily. You can achieve this by avoiding complex wording, grouping similar ideas, and not packing too much information into a single sentence. If you make it too long or complex to read, your reader will skip right over it.

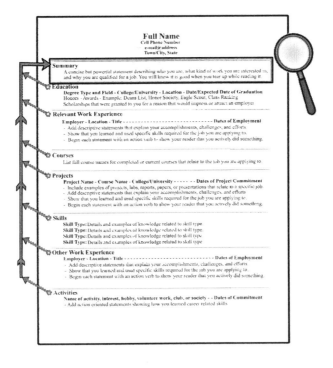

Summary Statement Content

Within this statement you should summarize your most relevant qualifications and career objectives.

1. **Qualifications**: Background, Personality traits, Skills, Experience

2. **Career Objectives**: Specific interests and specific criteria you are looking for in the job.

Helpful questions to ask yourself:
- What makes me successful?
- What defines me as a professional or how do I want to be defined?
- What is the most important qualification that matches my experience?
- What qualities differentiate me from other applicants?

Summary Statement Example

A summary that needs-improvement looks like:
    I am a college student looking for a job working as an engineer. I am a quick learner and am known around my class as having the best mathematical skill-set suited for professional work, I love reading books. I think I would like to design products at your company.

What needs to improve?
 This statement may make you sound like a nice person, but it's not going to make the applicant stand out to an employer as a front running candidate:

•Avoid generic and obvious statements, e.g. "I am a college student looking for a job working as an engineer."
•Avoid using first person ("I", "my").
•Avoid run on sentences and abrupt changes in flow and thought.

Summary Statement Example

A well-written summary looks like:

    Passionate about empathy-based design. Continuously developing a college-level skill-set in rapid prototyping, CAD development, and real world problem solving. Professional experience with mechanical component design in the defense industry.

What makes this summary well written?
The statement has a well-structured flow. It allows the reader to pick up key elements just by scanning it quickly, helping you stand out in a crowd:

- 2-3 Sentences (clear and concise).
- Creatively matches the writer's personality and top selling points with an employer's needs.
- Easy to scan for key qualifications, but doesn't feel like a forced list of keywords, or like you just copied over a job description.

Chapter 9
FEEDBACK

Your responsiveness to feedback will define who you are

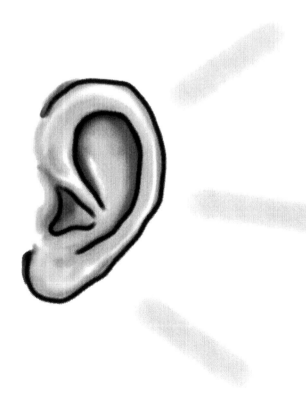

Get Feedback Early and Often

What was the first thing you wanted to do after writing your 12-minute resume? Show someone? Why? Because you know writing a successful resume requires feedback.

However, just gathering feedback is not enough to write a perfect resume. You must know when and where to get it, invest time analyzing it, and then use that analysis to improve the current state of your resume. Implementing this process is a sign of maturity; it takes practice, skill, and thick skin. But, if you can master it, the sky is the limit.

While getting feedback you will benefit from keeping an open mind and empathizing with other people's points of view. Even if it means having your most precious achievements face scrutiny, any feedback you receive is an opportunity to make improvements before an employer reads your resume.

Resume Feedback System

Use the simple feedback system below to develop your resume. Repeat this formula as many times as you need, until you feel confident in your resume. Then submit your polished resume to an employer.

1. Build Resume;
2. Get Feedback (Test);
3. Learn from Feedback;
Repeat.

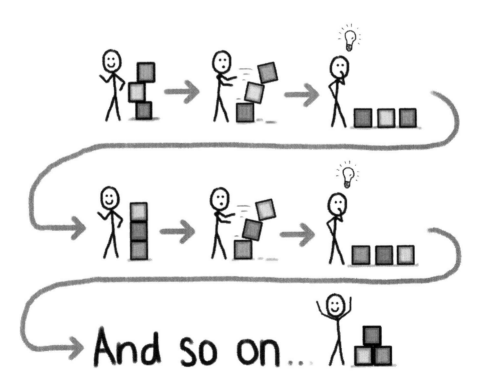

Make Time

The best way to get feedback on your resume is to do it in person. In order to do this, you may need to schedule your time around the time of others. Don't force people to give feedback, but instead try to find people who want to help you.

When you do find someone who is willing to help, they are more likely to commit if you communicate a specific meeting time. For example, "Would you mind spending 20 minutes at 10:30am to give me resume feedback?" This also helpful, because if they can't make the commitment you can ask them when would be a better time.

Prepare

If your feedback session is unplanned you may not have a chance to prepare. If you do have the luxury of planning ahead, make sure you find a workspace that is comfortable for both you and your reviewer to critique your resume. Sit at a table where you can be at about an arm's length from each other. Print out an extra copy of your resume and the job description to which you are applying. Remove any distractions: put away phones, unnecessary devices, and shut off the TV.

Focus on Small Chunks

Providing feedback on a full resume can be overwhelming for some people. To keep them focused, you can ask people to edit it in small chunks. This method allows the reader to only have to focus on one piece of content at a time. Move through each chunk of content together. Provide your reader with a starting and stopping point, and then review the content within those constraints before moving to the next chunk.

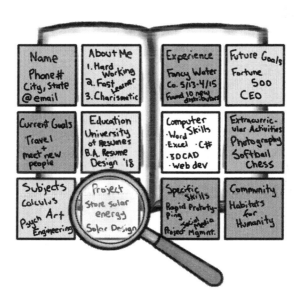

Ask Questions

3 Simple Feedback Questions:

What should I add?

- What do you think I'm missing?
- Why do you think it's important I add this?
- Why shouldn't I add this?

What should I remove?

- Do you think I should take this out?
- Why do you think I should remove this?
- What should I keep? Why?

What should I change?

- Do you think I should change this?
- Why do you think I should change this?
- Why shouldn't I change this?

Filter for You

You have the final word as to what goes in and what doesn't go in your resume. If you don't want to change something in your resume, don't do it. It is important that you only use your feedback to make changes that help you feel confident about your final resume.

Trust your gut, but also remember to take into account the experience, successes, and failures of your advisors.

Find Support

You are not alone on your path to starting your career. You are responsible for how you get there, but there are many supporters that want to help you along the way.

Your family, friends, professors, university career center, alumni, and even complete strangers want you to succeed. Accept their help and seek them out. Learn from their feedback and implement any changes that will improve your resume.

The next five pages profile different types of people who you might ask for feedback to help you recognize quality feedback opportunities and avoid feedback bias.

College Career Advisor

Your college career advisor should become your new best friend. They make a living advising other people just like you! They are going to base their advice off of historical evidence: what has worked in the past vs. what hasn't.

Be prepared to ask 'why?' Advisors edit resumes every day, and can easily make the mistake of assuming you know more than you do. Remember helping you, helps them.

Previous Employer

Your old bosses know your professional character better than anyone. They will be able to enlighten you on how others perceive your professional habits and abilities. The conversation might be awkward and uncomfortable, but learn from it, and turn it into a positive revision. They may even agree to be a reference for you.

The Pro

"The Pro" is a person that has built a career in the profession you want to apply for. This profile could describe a specific family member, family friend, or business acquaintance. Don't take their feedback personally. They have professional experience and can provide you with "big thinking", straight-forward, minimally biased feedback. The best way to approach the Pro is by having them focus on content and not on proof-reading. Ask them to prioritize what they think are your most important qualifications.

For Hire Resources

Another great way to catch spelling and grammar mistakes or get feedback on your resume are Online hiring services. Use websites like fiverr.com to hire people to proofread or provide feedback on your resume. Sites like this are great for college students because you can get feedback on your resume for low cost, with a fast turn-around time. It is wise to try out a few different editors and find one that you like. Not only is this a great way to get feedback but it also gives you experience hiring and managing someone to get something you want as well!

The Cynic

The cynic is your secret weapon. It is the person with whom you aren't sure why you're friends, because they are an asshole. But they will give it to you straight. They have high expectations not only for themselves, but everyone around them, which translates well when you need someone to criticize your resume.

Don't fall too far into their pessimistic trap. When they tell you something sucks, smile inside. You may have just found a change that leads you to your next job. Remember to absorb their feedback, listen, don't interrupt, and don't get offensive. If you hold the position as the bigger person, you can significantly profit from this exchange.

The Optimist

Beware of the optimist. We like to fall into the optimist's trap because positive feedback feels good. I'm not saying don't feel good about positive feedback, just know that some people will try to avoid confrontation, and will tell you what they think you want to hear. Recognize the courage of those who might be brave enough to disclose feedback that may hurt your feelings.

Take Action

What are you waiting for? You have your first resume. Remove your embarrassment filter, get off the couch, and challenge yourself! Go out and ask someone those precious 3 feedback questions: remove, add, or change. Keep your eyes wide, your ears alert, your mind open, and your pen ready. You've got this.

Leave the laziness to your roommate.

Chapter 10
REVIEW & SUBMIT

It's too late to chicken out now!

Resume Confidence

Let's reflect, at this point you will have almost reached your goal: submitting your resume to apply for a job. Up to now you have:

01. Built a resume prototype
02. Learned the basic resume sections, and expanded your content for each.
03. Learned how to properly research a job and employer and customize your resume to match relevant content to their needs.
04. Added detail to content you have selected.
05. Formatted your resume and added a summary statement
06. Received feedback

Now it's time to break through the roadblock that many run into: actually pressing the "SUBMIT" button.

Review Flow

Your reader should be able to read through your resume from top to bottom without having to stop or re-read any sentences. Employers view the latter as an indicator of poor communication skills. They expect to only have to read a sentence once to understand it, and generally do not have the time or patience to do otherwise. Blatant mistakes in your resume can quickly earn your application a rejection status depending on an employer's tolerance for error.

Flow Exercise:

Read your resume out loud before submitting it. This exercise will give you an opportunity to discover if anything sounds "off-key". If you have to stop and re-read something, you probably need to make an edit.

File Format

When you submit your resume use a .PDF format if possible. This is a universally accepted format that converts your word-processing document into an image file of your resume. This is important because it won't negatively affect your format if the employer tries to convert your resume from your original word-processor document file type to a different one.

When you name your file include the date, your name, and the job name.
For Example:
Resume_Matthew Cross_Internship_03.21.2015.pdf

Always check your converted file's format. Sometimes converting your document can unintentionally extend your resume onto a second page. Ensure that your employer reads your resume as it was intended.

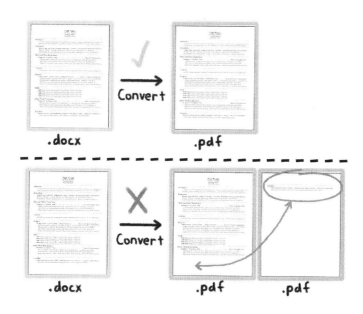

Review Checklist

- [ ] **01** I have researched the employer and job description and have selected the content I feel will give me the best chance at getting hired to use in my resume.

- [ ] **02** I feel comfortable talking about my resume content in an interview with an employer.

- [ ] **03** My summary statement is clear concise and error free.

- [ ] **04** I have reviewed all of the recommendations from my feedback, and either decided to include or ignore the comments.

- [ ] **05** I have read my final draft out loud, paying special attention to grammar, spelling, and avoiding using "I" or repetitive word choices.

- [ ] **06** I have reviewed the actual file that I am submitting to the employer to ensure there are no formatting errors during conversion.

- [ ] **07** I am ready.

Submit: Take Initiative

Submit your resume directly to an employer or recruiter in response to a job description. A proactive approach includes sending an e-mail directly to a hiring manager, applying through a company's website, or applying Online through a 3rd party job search website.

For internships and entry level jobs employers find it more efficient to be reactive to applicants who show interest in a position, rather than seeking out someone who may have the right qualifications but no interest in the job.

Submit: Timing

Apply to a job opportunity as soon as it becomes available. Don't wait. The earlier you are on the employer's list of applicants, the more likely they are to read your resume.

On the contrary, as long as a job is still posted that means the position hasn't been filled. If a job post lingers for a significant amount of time the employer may start to become willing to compromise on some of their expectations.

Make sure you submit your resume on a weekday, when the hiring manager is at work and more likely to give it attention.

File Organization

Taking time to manage each version of your resume is a great way to learn from your past, and save time and improve in the future. Use a free cloud based file management system like Dropbox, Google Drive, or Microsoft OneDrive to allow yourself access to your resumes anywhere you can get the Internet. Use the following example to help organize your folder structure, and store the appropriate information:

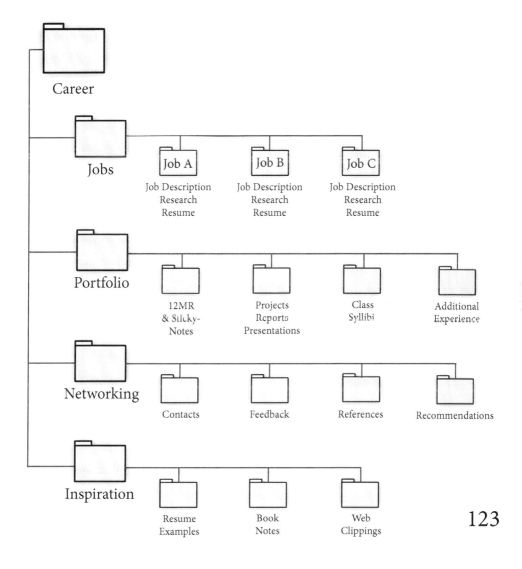

Your Public Profile

There is an ever expanding number of opportunities that develop under the umbrella of your Online public profile. The results that show up when you search your name using Google can either be your best friend or your worst nightmare. Be ready for when your resume reader looks you up. Make sure that things Online that you want to stay private, stay private, and that your public profile supplements your resume in a beneficial way. Focus on social media sites such as LinkedIn, Twitter, Facebook, and Google to build your brand, and re-iterate the type of person you want an employer to discover you as.

Unlike your one page resume, Online profiles provide you almost unlimited space to post information about yourself. Treat your public profile as if it were an extension of your resume. By public profile I mean anything that shows up as representing you on the Internet: Twitter, Facebook, Google, etc.

Create a Linked In profile. When doing this, instead of using a specific job description to select the information you want to provide, you want to go for bulk. List as much about yourself as you can. There are no limits.

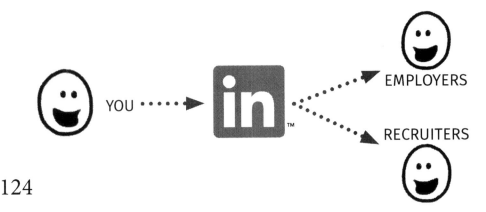

Be a Leader

Inspire others to give their resume the attention it deserves. This book was designed to help you learn many new concepts; share those concepts! Give friends and classmates an open invitation to give you their resume for feedback, and follow through when asked. Use the resume development tools you have learned to help others find a new perspective, and help them build enough confidence to hit their own submit button. By helping others write their resumes, you can reinforce what you learned from this book, and also can learn from their techniques to continue improving your own resume writing skills.

Believe in Yourself

You have a resume in your hands, brains in your head, and a heart in your chest. Take the path less traveled and learn from your mistakes. Don't just let life happen around you; control your future. Learn to ask questions, set small goals, and dream of big ones. Absorb any criticism and let it fuel you. Convince others that you are worthy of your dream, and show them that you are willing to put up a damn good fight for it. Believe in the story of you.

Acknowledgments

Thank you to these special few who donated their time to read and provide in-depth feedback during the development of this book (even when it was just a few sticky-notes on a wall).

Jennifer Seavey
Heidi Cross
Tom Nilsson
Austin Cormier
H. Joseph Drapalski & Anet Castro
Cheryl Brooks
Bill Pacheco
Cameron McLeod
Van Latham
Michael Fisher
Charlie & Ellen McDonald
Ayesha Dadabhoy

About the Author

Matthew Cross has been a dreamer since he was a boy. While growing up in Franklin, MA he gravitated towards his love of art. However, he was convinced that he'd never earn a living as a professional artist. He chose to pursue a career in mechanical engineering, where he could translate his passion for art through mechanical design.

During his years in the College of Engineering at the University of Massachusetts in Amherst, he worked two internships.: one in environmental engineering, and another in systems engineering, designing components for nuclear submarine optronic masts contracted by the U.S. Navy.

As college graduation loomed, one of the worst economic declines since the Great Depression put the job market on freeze. While working at the university's Engineering Career and Development Center, Matthew and his classmates were uncertain of what their future would hold. Under the tutelage of Director Cheryl Brooks, he spent much of his time helping his friends and classmates write resumes and prepare for interviews in the midst of a barren college job market. It was this difficult time, while he and his fellow classmates struggled to find jobs in their field, that prepared Matthew to write this book.

After graduating, Matthew spent a year at a job in Silicon Valley designing products for a Medical Device Start-up. He then moved back to Boston and has spent the past four years designing commercial fitness equipment and their manufacturing processes for Cybex International.

Matthew currently lives in Newton, MA with his girlfriend Jennifer and works as a mechanical engineer for Cybex. He is the son of Tom and Heidi Cross, brother of Katelyn Cross, and grandson of Albert Hutton. Matthew is a descendant of the Hendy Family of Sunnyvale, CA and the great-grand nephew of Wilber L Cross of New Haven, Connecticut.

Made in the USA
Lexington, KY
01 May 2015